For the light of my life...my mother

In the middle of nothingness, in the labyrinth of this void,
Alleging the ruthless world, I think I realised,
There was a theory rather fact I was hiding from myself,
That the world can't be held accountable for the plight of thyself.
That moment, that instance I tried to gather some courage,
For this time, ego had to be the convict and the soul had to judge.
The question posed was to the ones telling to beware of the world full of evils,
When will they teach us to keep the world safe from ourselves?

Resting my head below millions of stars,
In such calm yet wild hours ,
When I find myself alone with my fantasies that only I see
I profoundly wish I had a me with me.

Walking though the lanes where memories are confined,
In such loud yet silent times,
When I find myself lost with words that only I perceive ,
I profoundly wish I had a me with me.

Stepping out in rain to douse the flames of present,
In such blissful yet miserable seconds,
When I find myself amidst the joy that only I feel,
I profoundly wish I had a me with me.

Writing my expressions which confine just within my clan,
In such poetic yet literal span,
When I find myself cherishing words that only I can read ,
I profoundly wish I had a me with me.

Listening to the music from soul that defines my existence ,
In such soothing yet agitating instances,
When I find myself with tunes that only I can sing,
I profoundly wish I had a me with me.

Trying to find a me for myself,
In such tiring yet worthy timelessness,
When I find myself in search of me that only I want to be,
I profoundly wish I had a me with me.

A ME FOR MYSELF

The tale arises from the valley of mountains,
Where Noor and Alizeh lived along the banks of river Jehlum.
To explore the unexplored, they took a trek to the woods.
With endless talks and laughter in the air,
They kept walking towards the misery awaiting them ahead.

As the sky turned dark and the air grew cold,
Noor and Alizeh could feel jitters run down their bones.
The two friends took steps unaware of their fate,
As path so wide seemed narrowing towards emptiness.

Noor heard some voices so unfamiliar as Alizeh tried to calm her down,
Both felt the darkness trying to communicate the warning.
Yet they kept going foreseeing the signs.

The evening seemed to consume the two,
When a dark figure appeared in front of them.
Loud thunders echoed through the forest
As the rain descended to greet the horror surrounding the woods.

There seemed a light approaching them,
It was their nightmare disguised as hope.
But as it came nearer towards the two
It revealed the terror that was yet to come.

Noor murmured, "goodbye forever" as a tear rolled down Alizeh's eye,
The figure spread through the sky concealing their screams.
As horror captured the helpless friends,
The mountains mourned the loss of yet another lives.

Noor and Alizeh were never seen again,
Their tale lost in the darkness, consumed by pain
That evening so wretched revealed nothing to the world,
As the woods kept their secret forever to remain.

THE TALE OF THAT EVENING

Life feels like a bunch of funerals,
Funerals of everything I could have been.
It is like witnessing thousands of deaths,
Deaths of all the lives I could have lived.

I am tired of writing eulogies for my happiness,
It dies brutal deaths every second.
I have run out of shrouds for my hope,
As I use them to strangle it more than to cover its remains.

The fire no more agrees to light the pyre of my fears,
As I witness my misery playing with its flames.
It only burns my will to escape,
Escape the graveyard of loneliness that surrounds me

I eagerly await the day I'll bury this nothingness,
The day saying goodbye to this void won't be so hard.
It will be like growing flowers on their graves,
To nourish a new life on the casket of the dead.

EULOGY FOR LIFE

Often when I am curled up in my nest,
the wind asks me what grief feels like.
Is it feeling lonely amidst the crowd,
or does it feel like a knife slitting your throat?

I smile at the naive wind,
for it has tormented hundreds of cities,
and ripped off thousands of leaves,
and yet it thinks of grief as pain.

Grief feels like being without a blanket on a chilly evening,
It's like a ship navigating a tempest unguarded.
Grief is witnessing the wind destroy the nest.
And seeing once a lively river, dry up.

Grief feels like approaching autumn after a lively summer,
It is entering a house that is not home
Grief is sleeping with nightmares that are seen with open eyes,
It feels like not witnessing the moon on a starry night.

WHAT GRIEF FEELS LIKE

It is my heart that aches,
Looking at the mirror.
Is it your pale skin or your empty eyes,
That you despise, the mirror asks.

I shroud this evil in darkness,
For I might look at any sight but my own.
It laughs at my cowardice,
I laugh at its delusions.

Then one fine day I confront it and scream,
It's not my eyes or skin that I hate.
I revile the ugliness inside of me.
I detest the face of my soul.

The mirror shows me my worse I wish to conceal,
I shatter it to be liberated forever.
It laughs at my fears,
As I stare at its pieces with an empty gaze.

MIRROR MIRROR ON THE WALL

It's yet another day,
I am struggling to send the invaders away.
My mind although loves to tame them,
But it can't feed them anymore.

But then I realize I am unarmed,
I can't fight these all alone.
My hands start trembling...I feel numb,
I tried not to, but here I lye anxious all again.

These visitors cause me a great deal of pain,
They bring fear, guilt, regret,loss and ugliness.
I tell them to leave, I swear I do,
But they keep returning, as if Iam a home to them.

So I keep starving my mind to feed them,
Hoping someday they'll get tired of me.
They'll leave me alone to fetch some light,
Although I might do what they taught me...choose to befriend the dark.

INTRUSIVES

When I am old and worn out,
My Freckles visible from a mile.
Skin weathered and pale,
And silver strands adorn me regally.

Sitting in my lawn, what will I recall?
Fortunes I made, or gold I earned.
Shall my mind wander to towering empires,
Or luxury left in my wake?

Though I might not be wise even then
But with certainty I must say,
In the momens I'm alone, I'll hold dear
The ripples of smile I've spread.

The echoes of laugher I recieved.
Moments that were precious in memory,
Acts of kindness bestowed and returned,
And all the people I have loved.

WHEN I AM OLD

Oh to be brave on a rainy day,
Is not to shelter under an umbrella.
To embrace bravery on a downpour.
Is to be drenched and soaked to the core.

To be happy on a gloomy evening,
Is not to supress the silence by melodies.
To find joy on a hopeless twilight,
Is to stare at the blank sky with no respite.

To be warm on a chilly night,
Is not to curl in a blanket.
To feel the warmth in the night's embrace,
Is to feel the breeze blowing the hair.

To be hopeful on a miserable day,
Is not to hope for a better tomorrow.
To truely hold onto hope when life is grey,
Is not to surrender to the misery, come what may.

TO BE BRAVE ON A RAINY DAY

As I walk through the corridors of the hospital
I can see the paradox its rooms hold.
Happy faces blessed with children,
To faces mourning loses of their lives.

The halls have seen hope and despair,
The windows have witnessed love and loss collide.
The floors on which battles of fragile lives are fought,
The walls have heard wispers of counteless prayers.

Amidst pain, people holding on to faith,
Between restless dawns and happy dusks .
Life and death walks hand in hand with grace
For hope's fragile thread to find its place.

THE PARADOXICAL HOSPITALS

I was wondering if I could ever tell you,
That I no more love things that captivate others.
Rather I often find myself adoring things,
That are acclaimed for being abhorred.

The bright sunshine no more thrills me,
Nor does that warm shower of rain.
The blazing heat of sun now gives me solace
So does that startling sound of thunder.

The lively spring has lost its colours,
And autumn is now just a grave of leaves.
The cold winter gives me warmth now,
And dry rivers of summer quench my thirst.

Sky shows me stars losing their light,
All I can see in moon is its prominent scars.
Abandoned rocks have caught my eye,
The broken chunks in sky now feel like home.

I wonder if I would ever tell you all this,
That I no more cherish the things that fascinate others.
For you and the world may never understand,
That if beauty is meant to be protected then vulnerabilities are supposed to be loved.

THE RUINS FEEL LIKE HOME

Deep in shadows where darkness thrived,
A voice emerged, seemed like death arrived.
It whispered gently to my jaded soul,
Begged me with all its might, to once again be whole.

With my nothingness surrounding me like a shroud,
I could barely pay heed to death's sacred requests.
It reminded me I was mortal and would eventually meet my fate,
But I still have time to embrace all the good that is still left.

In the realm of silence and decay,
Life yearns for life, to find its way.
To witness the warmth of morning sun,
And to light up at the sight of stars at midnight.

So why can't you rise from your depths of misery,
Even when the gloomy skies have some peace to offer
To seek slightest of light in the darkest of nights.
And find comfort in life's bittersweet embrace.

Cherish each heartbeat as a song of courage,
Weave tapestry of your stories that were untold.
Let the gentle lullabies of triumph and defeat put you to sleep.
Fear not the voids inside you that drain your soul.

When your last breath will paint its final scene on your canvas,
It should be as colorful and bright as you have been
Death came as a companion to teach me my lessons of life,
Pleaded me to live so that it can take me alive...

WHEN DEATH CAME TO BEG

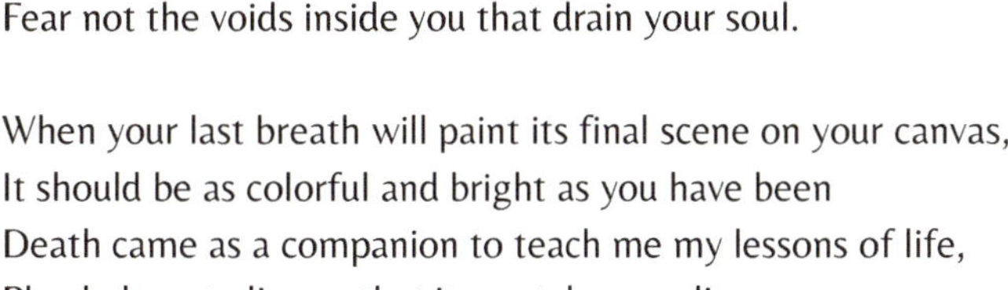

As I stare out of my window on a rainy day,
My mind wanders back to the old happy days.
When I used to await impatiently for the season that I abhor now,
Just to pack my bags and leave for the city of gold.

I remember walking through the bustling bazaars,
The aroma of sweets that spread through the air,
The colorful shops with pretty bangles,
And the crowd moving through roads that seemed divine.

I can recall my eagerness to sit in the rickshaws,
The roofs of which could be seen gleaming in the sun.
The walks that we took in the evening,
To relish sweets amidst the chilly breeze.

The voices of vendors, cars and the soothing hymes still echo in my ears,
As I hold on to the reminiscents of my childhood days.
As I see the new streets which are unrecognizable now,
I stroll through my memories to find peace in the old streets that seemed my own.

The big statutes, new shops, fancy lights may be captivating to people,
But my heart will always love the old broken shops and untilled roads.
That are now nowhere to be seen or found,
Just like my old interests that I have outgrown.

As I stare outside my window on a usual rainy day,
My mind wanders back to the winters of 2012,
When we created memories that now seem so blur,
Amidst the hustle and bustle of the precious streets of Amritsar.

AMRITSAR STREETS

My head hurts and so do my eyes,
but does anyone care just to look by?
My heart aches for a blissful gaze,
My soul is setting all the saved joy ablaze.

How do I stop things from falling apart?
Save memories of people, places and everything precious I lost ?
Is there a way out of this maize of ache?
My tears ask me each time they struggle to escape.

The broken pieces of my heart have now started to hurt me,
Some piercing into my soul to leave scars concealing all the glee,
An abyss of thoughts keeps haunting me at nights,
The pyre of my words has been lit using the flame of my plight.

This nothingness which was neither blissful nor full of pain,
Is now turning into an aching void, my mind can't tame.
My own shadow is now fed up of my darkness,
My own evils now try to escape my domain so vicious.

Everyday a new mountain of fear and agony is built inside me,
The rocks of which will be turned into a new depiction of bravery.
Everyday a new fire of self loath and hate is burned inside me,
The ashes of which I will turn into a new portrayal of artistry.

ASHES INTO ART

I was lying on the fragile floor of my numbness,
When I heard a voice so familiar yet unusual,
I searched for it, where voices and words are rarely found,
 Just to realise it was a call from the inside of me.

 All my fears, fed up of my fear asked me to confront them,
Afraid they too were of the fading light, being replaced by aura so darker.
I didn't want to supress them as if they were just an illusion.
So one after the other they spoke to remind me their existence.

The fear that sent jitters down my spine was first to be heard,
It charged me of nourishing it, when I could have destroyed its roots.
I let fear of their death overpower the value of their presence to me,
 I had no answers for this "fear of losing people" as it begged me to lose it.

The fear I wished I never encountered came next,
it convicted me of losing my courage so unbreakable over it.
I watered it to make the value of rising an oblivion for me,
I couldn't deny the allegations of this "fear of falling" as it begged me to rise above it.

The fear that made me cold was the next to visit,
It accused me of taking scars instead of warmth rising from it.
I feared the nightmares of worldly flames, unaware of the ones burning inside me,
I accepted the curses of this " fear of fire" as it begged me to make ashes of it.

The fear that knocked next was an illusion, yet so strong,
It blamed me of letting it make me so vulnerable to all fears.
I was scared by the thought of being left alone amidst the crowds of thoughts,
I apologised to this "fear of loneliness" as it begged me learn to live without it.

As all my fears slept peacefully in the blanket of my misery that night,
My eyes kept staring at the emptiness surrounding me.
The thought of all the charges had just began to pierce my soul,
 Just when I heard the "fear of living without any fears" knock my abode.

WHAT MY FEARS FEARED

To the leaves that get parted from the trees,
How do you bear the pain of separation?
Every time wind rips you part from heights,
How do you accept the betrayal in darkness?

To the trees that soak sunshines with leaves,
How do you abandon them for ruthless autumn?
Every time they drape their lively red shroud,
Do you not mourn their beauty so lifeless?

To the wind that shows no mercy to the leaves,
Do you never curse your soul so frigid?
Every time soil begs you for liberation from lifelessness
Do you not pity it turning into a grave of leaves?

To the sky that witnesses the gruesome bloodshed,
Do you never beg the nature for justice?
Every time a life is perished in your embrace,
Do you never shed tears for its fate?

To the creator who never convicts nature for the murders,
How do you forgive and foresee its crimes?
Every time a leaf is rip apart into pieces,
Is it you who turns blind towards its own creations?

THE MURDER

I sometimes feel if the fireflies could talk,
They would tell me how much they detest the moon,
For fascination should be for something that's real.
But it steals their charm, by the light that's not even its own.

They would shout and scream and tell the world,
To prevent their oblivion that will blend with timelessness,
For they would be shining the brightest among the woods,
But the eyes would still be devoted to the light that's foreign.

The stars may calm them and lend them their shoulder,
For moon also overpowers a part of their marvel.
A beautiful acquaintance over light may thus be formed.
But the world would say,
"too much of a light blinds them" and still persist to admire the moon.

IF FIREFLIES COULD TALK

Have you ever keenly observed the fire?
How brutally it cries while it burns.
Have you ever noticed how it betrays itself?
Making friends with water when it comes to the one it sheds.

Have you ever seen it detesting its own flames?
How badly it curses them each time they shatter something.
Have you ever perceived how it abhors its entity?
Each time it fails to offer warmth and gives burns instead.

Have you ever noted its hopelessness?
How helpless it feels when anything that comes close, reduces to ashes.
Have you ever sensed how empty it feels?
Coming across the awful scars it leaves.

Next time you go near the poor fire,
Remember to emphasize with it,
Because aren't we all fire too,
just unapologetic about being it ?

THE MISERY OF FIRE

The ambience that once was a home to the sufis,
The society that once propagated the doctrine of love and humanity,
The domain that once beautified itself with its warmth and compassion,
Is today witnessing itself drowning in blood.

The valley that was once regarded as the 'Pir Vaer',
The fraternity that once laid its pillars on 'Ikhlas' and Unity,
The order that was considered to be the warmest of all,
Is today witnessing all its principals fading away in hostility.

The mountains that once echoed the chants of "Lal-Vaakh" and "Sufiana Kalam",
The rivers that once carried the blissful messages of "Sahazanand",
The winds that once whispered the idea of
oneness,
Are today witnessing its rich past dying in chaos.

As I watch my home that is home no more,
As I watch Harmukh looking down at me with compassion no more,
As I watch my Jehlum willing to offer me its sanctuary no more,
My heart cries out for the Chinar bleeding for its leaves that are on it no more.

THE CHINAR IS BLEEDING

There is a lighthouse across the ocean,
That awaits its ship in the midst of the cold night,
When the moon rests in the blanket of the ocean,
And the world is at peace,quiet and asleep.

The ship keeps itself safe for the lighthouse,
From loud thunderstorms and deadly waves.
The ship that endured storms now fears them,
For it understands that it owes its life for the lighthouse.

The ocean laughs on the plight of the ship,
The sailor regards it as a coward.
The moon being wise edifies it,
Amidst a storm, ships never hope they'll return to the shore.

The lighthouse lights up to suppress it's agitation,
All it does and is capable of, is to wait.
For they have found peace in unpredictability,
And that's what the greatest of courages takes it to do.

THE SHIP AND THE LIGHTHOUSE

I adore the days when it rains,
For the tiny droplets douse all the corporal flames.
I adore the days when the waters descends from the skies,
For they quench the thirst of all the unspoken lies.
I adore the days when the clouds arrive,
For they give the affection in which the blossoms thrive.
I adore the days when the thunder sounds are heard,
For they aid to suppress all the corporal words.
I adore the days when the sky lightens up with sparks,
For they leave behind something other than unsolicited marks.
I adore the days when the rain descends to embrace my soul,
For it gifts me the calmness for which my mind always strolls

WHEN IT RAINS

We never had a forever,
nor would there have been one,
But please listen to my lie maybe it gives you peace,
it could have been a forever just if we would have known ourselves a bit more

We never had an infinity
nor would there have been one,
But please give a ear to my lie maybe it gives you bliss,
it could have been an infinity just if we would have stared the same sky a bit more.

We never had an eternity
nor would there have been one,
But please hear my lie maybe it heals your wounds,
it could have been an eternity just if we would have talked about us a bit more.

We never had a great beyond
nor would there have been one,
But please pay heed to my lie maybe it gives you comfort,
It could have been a great beyond just if we would have been out of this labyrinth a bit more.

We never had a happily ever after
nor would there have been one,
But please perceive my lie maybe it gives you ease,
it could have been a happily ever after just if we would have forgiven us a bit more.

We never had a forever
nor would there have been one,
But please take in my lie maybe it gives you solace,
it could have been a forever, an infinity, an eternity, a great beyond
and even a happily ever after
just if we knew what these catchy words actually meant a bit more.

LIES I TELL MYSELF

I still remember those scary nights,
Just days after the storm was over
When the sounds of thunder kept haunting me
Making me shed tears for the boat I lost.

I can still recall those dreadful times,
Just days after I had said goodbye to my boat
The anxiety of facing another hurricane kept me awake at nights,
Making me worried for the only oar I was left with.

I wanted to leave the nightmares behind,
I wished to cross the remaining ocean with my oar
But the flashbacks kept terrifying my soul to its core.
I was left alone and helpless amidst the vast ocean.

That is when I helped myself by being you,
I talked days and nights to myself ny being you.
As time passed I realized my fears were vanishing.
You were helping me heal, you helped me sleep.

You made me stronger than I was,
I was no more terrified by the thought of another hazard.
I felt I could face storms, thunders come what may,
To show you, how your delusional presence healed my soul.

I may never be able to say this to you,
For you might think I am a lunatic.
But I will forever be grateful for your delusional existence.
I will be grateful
For the one who helped me heal, To the one who helped me sleep...
.

TO THE ONE WHO HELPED ME SLEEP